Movie Publicity Showcase Volume 6

Laurel and Hardy in "Thicker Than Water" and Other Shorts

I. Joseph Hyatt

To purchase books in quantity for fund raising, classroom use or to use as incentives email HVCScrapbook@aol.com.

Copyright © 2015 I. Joseph Hyatt

All rights reserved.

ISBN: 1518762085
ISBN-13: 978-1518762086

DEDICATION

To all the people who worked on the films in front of and behind the cameras. To all the people who worked in the offices creating the publicity. To all the people that helped in the distribution and exhibition of this movie. To all the people working today to preserve and make available classic films to the public.

To the members of the Sons of the Desert, the Laurel and Hardy Appreciation Society, for helping to keep the films of Laurel and Hardy alive.

To my wife Mary who has put up with my old movie obsession all these years.

To David Lord Heath, Gino Dercola and Roger Robinson for their help in bringing this series of books together with its audience.

To Mark Eisler and his family and to Cliff Sawyer, just for being a phone call away.

ACKNOWLEDGMENTS

"Thicker Than Water" is the final short film starring Laurel and Hardy. Directed by James W. Horne, produced by Hal Roach, and released in 1935 by Metro Goldwyn Mayer, the short also features James Finlayson and Daphne Pollard in supporting roles.

"Beau Hunks" is the only four reel short Laurel and Hardy film, directed by James W. Horne, and featuring Charles Middleton, Tiny Sanford, and Charlie Hall. It was produced by Hal Roach, and released in 1931 by Metro Goldwyn Mayer.

"Perfect Day" was directed by James Parrott and featured Laurel and Hardy, along with Edgar Kennedy, Kay Deslys, and Isabelle Keith. MGM released this early sound Hal Roach two-reel short in 1929.

"Blotto" is a three-reel short staring Laurel and Hardy, directed by James Parrott, produced by Hal Roach, and released in 1930 by MGM.

"County Hospital" is a two reel short made in 1932. It was directed by James Parrott, produced by Hal Roach and distributed by MGM. It featured Laurel and Hardy with Billy Gilbert.

"Berth Marks" is the second sound film featuring Laurel and Hardy. Released in 1929 in two reels, it was directed by Lewis R. Foster, produced by Hal Roach and distributed by MGM.

"Come Clean" is a 1931 Laurel and Hardy two reel short. It was directed by James W. Horne, produced by Hal Roach and distributed by MGM.

These movies are shown on Turner Classic Movies Channel in the US. Check listings at TCM.com for show times. In the United States and Canada, at the time of this writing, these films are available as part of the 10 disc DVD set "Laurel & Hardy: The Essential Collection" from Vivendi Entertainment. In the United Kingdom and Europe these shorts are available in "Laurel and Hardy: The Collection", released by Universal Pictures UK. They are also available on separate discs. All of these can be found wherever you buy your movies and books.

"Shiver My Timbers" is a 1931 Our Gang short (two reels) directed by Robert F. McGowan, produced by Hal Roach and distributed by MGM. It is available on Vivendi Entertainment's "The Little Rascals Volume 3."

"Nickel Nurser" is a two reel Charley Chase short released in 1932, produced by Hal Roach and distributed by MGM. Directed by Warren Doane, this film features Billy Gilbert and Thelma Todd. It is not yet available on DVD.

The following press book reproductions will help bring you back to the films' 1930's releases. I hope you enjoy this book and the films mentioned within.

I. Joseph Hyatt
October 25, 2015

INTRODUCTION FROM VOLUME 1
MOVIE PUBLICITY SHOWCASE: LAUREL & HARDY IN "SWISS MISS"

For many "old time" movie fans that grew up in the sixties and seventies, television gave us our first exposure to classic films. In a day before video tape recorders, cable, streaming, DVD, Blu-ray, and computers we considered ourselves lucky when one of our favorite movies was broadcast. With the exception of the CBS annual broadcast of "The Wizard of Oz" and stations such as New York's WOR that ran one movie (Million Dollar Movie) eleven times a week, an average movie would probably air twice in a five year period.

However there was an exception. A large one, mainly aimed for a children's audience. You could find movie series like "The East Side Kids/Bowery Boys", "Laurel and Hardy", "Abbott and Costello" and low budget horror movies weekly airing every Saturday. Under group titles such as "East Side Comedy" or "Chiller Theater" weekly showings of many of these favorites were more visible than the serious or classic films.

WPIX's Officer Joe Bolton presented the Three Stooges daily.

Chuck McCann with the Paul Ashley Puppets.

Early ad for Chuck McCann's daily show.

The Little Rascals/Our Gang were funny under any name.

Making the rounds of TV stations during this same period were a number of movie shorts collections, the most visible of these clusters being the Three Stooges, Laurel and Hardy and the Little Rascals/Our Gang. On many stations they were run with a live host. Chuck McCann, "Officer" Joe Bolton, Alan Swift and John Zacherley were hosts in the New York/New Jersey market. Other cities across the country had their own local hosts. Often these shows would broadcast Monday through Friday, and appear on the weekends as well.

Since we couldn't own a copy of the film as you can today, many of us tried to "capture" a bit of the emotions we felt by buying magazines, comics, toys, photos, and records with our favorite movie personalities. Sound tracks were recorded on our reel-to-reel audio tape recorders. Some of us even had a family home movie projector where you could buy a few minutes of older films and cartoons in 8mm silent (later sound) editions for a reasonable price (if we saved up our money and dad let us use the family projector). For most of us, a more professional film gauge was just an expensive dream.

Atlas Films - NYC

Carnival Films - NYC

Blackhawk Films - Davenport, Iowa

Now collectables like movie posters, photos, and other movie memorabilia are very expensive. Back in the 1960's and earlier theaters and movie distributors would recycle posters, photos and movie campaign books until the films reached the end of their theatrical showings. Then these paper items would be disposed of. The suppliers (like National Cinema Service) either threw out or gave these mementoes to anyone who would clear their warehouse. Stores like Marc Ricci's Memory Shop in New York City and many more acquired much of this material by the truckload. Before these items were considered collectable (or even worthy of preservation) we could purchase some of these photos, lobby cards, and posters between $1 - $7 each in stores like these, or through mail order.

Today many posters sell in the 5 and 6 figures range. Pre-1940 material is the most expensive, since many of the paper items were donated (and recycled) for the war effort. Today it takes a collector with "deep pockets" to afford some of the original material.

For movie lovers and students of film one of these prize collectables is the movie campaign book. Originally campaign books, more commonly referred to as "press books", were circulated to theaters during the film's distribution. They were used so the movie exhibitor could pick out the posters that would fit his theater front and to chose pre-written articles and ads to run in newspapers within the theater's advertising budget.

Without trying, press books ended up documenting the choice of posters, banners, photos and other promotional items that were available for future generations. Radio ads and ideas for lobby displays, publicity articles, newspaper ad artwork, and general information about the film was also documented within its pages.

This series of books, starting with "Movie Publicity Showcase - Volume One - Laurel and Hardy in Swiss Miss", have been put together to allow people to understand what it was like to be a patron (or theater manager) when these films were originally presented. It is also a source for other film students, writers, or the movie enthusiast to read items (some fact- some Hollywood fiction at its finest) that were written to make an audience desire to be in the movie's audience.

Most of the press books in this series are presented as they were originally printed with two exceptions. A common size for these press books was approximately 12" x 18" in size. While full pages were used to represent the cover, back and poster pages, articles had to be separated and enlarged to make reading possible in this 8.5" x 11" book format. The synopsis covering the story (which included the ending) has also been eliminated. These synopsizes were not intended for use in publicizing the movie and give away the total story, including the ending.

Many archives and movie studios are now actively restoring and preserving the remaining film and advertising elements that still exist today.

Whenever a movie in this series is available, I hope that reading the original publicity material will encourage you to seek out the title. For information on the film's availability and other important information about the film's preservation, refer to the acknowledgement section in the front of this book.

INTRODUCTION TO VOLUME 6
MOVIE PUBLICITY SHOWCASE: LAUREL & HARDY IN "THICKER THAN WATER" AND OTHER SHORTS

Much has been written in recent years about Stan Laurel and Oliver Hardy, their films, the studios they worked at, and the co-stars they performed with. Everything from their lives to their work has been well documented and analyzed.

The Movie Publicity Showcase Volumes were not printed to add new opinions, reviews, or critique to this body of work that is now available. It is meant to do the opposite by reprinting original materials from the films initial releases.

Instead of looking at the films from a twenty-first century perspective, the hope of this series is to enable the reader to experience the films through the eyes of a movie patron of the 1930's - 1940's.

There is material on seven Laurel and Hardy shorts in this volume. "Thicker Than Water," "Berth Marks" and "Come Clean" are represented by their original press sheets. "Beau Hunks," "Perfect Day," "Blotto," and "County Hospital" have original release articles that were reused for their 1937 reissues.

Also included are the original press sheets from Charley Chase's 1932 "The Nickel Nurser" and Our Gang's 1931 "Shiver My Timbers," both of which were made by Hal Roach Studios during this time period.

All the shorts are available for home viewing except "The Nickel Nurser." Sadly the work of Charley Chase at Hal Roach Studios have not been released to DVD. However, this film, along with other Chase films have been shown on Turner Classic Movies network, and continue to be a part of their line-up. Check local listings. The work of Charley Chase is worth the search.

A FURTHER NOTE: THE FILMS CLASSICS REISSUES

Film Classics (later Favorite Films) was a film distributor that specialized in movie reissues to theaters. It was formed in 1946 by Moe Kerman (of Astor Films, another distributor of reissued movies) along with J. J. Felder and Leo Seligman. They acquired the rights to redistribute Laurel and Hardy films theatrically. Film Classics, a low budget corporation, utilized as much publicity from the original release campaign as possible.

Film Classics did change the posters for the film. New one sheets, inserts, and lobby cards were quickly produced. With bright colors and new arrangements, the posters used for the reissue gave a newer, more modern look than the original 1930's material, even with the use of stock images. Within this book some of these reissue materials are reprinted.

The audiences in the theaters for these reissues saw a slightly different publicity package on the theater fronts, however they saw the same classic Laurel and Hardy films that have been entertaining comedy enthusiasts for over 8 decades.

The Film Classic releases replaced the original titles with their own, replacing M-G-M distribution credits.

HAL ROACH PRESENTS

STAN LAUREL and OLIVER HARDY

in

"THICKER THAN WATER"

with

DAPHNE POLLARD   **JAMES FINLAYSON**

Funnier Than Ever in New Comedy

Laurel and Hardy

"Thicker Than Water," Last Of Laurel-Hardy Two-Reel Comedies, Howling Affair

Laurel and Hardy, supported by an able cast, including Daphne Pollard, Jimmy Finlayson, Harry Bowen and other well-known comics, are seen in "Thicker Than Water," which comes to the . . . . Theatre next . . . . as the last two-reeler they will make under the Hal Roach banner. A new agreement calls for fun productions of four reels and full-feature length in the future.

"Thicker Than Water" marks finis to what was probably the most successful series of two-reel comedies ever produced since the advent of motion pictures. Jimmy Horne, who has directed Laurel and Hardy in many of their fun films since they were teamed seven years ago, and who handled the megaphone for their recent full-length feature, "Bonnie Scotland," directs this final short.

For more than seven years Laurel and Hardy have romped through two-reel pictures, only occasionally appearing in films of greater length. Now, the demand is so great for comedies of greater length as vehicles for the famous fun duo, that Hal Roach has decided to grant the public's request and in the future there will be no more two-reelers with this stellar combination.

"Thicker Than Water" concerns the domestic adventures of Mr. and Mrs. Hardy and their star boarder, Mr. Laurel. Daphne Pollard is seen as Ollie's diminutive wife. Jimmy Finlayson, veteran screen comic, has the role of an installment payment collector. It is the old story of who's to be boss of the family with complications supplied by the star boarder.

It is gratifying that this, their last two-reeler, is unquestionably one of the best Hal Roach-M-G-M comedy shorts Laurel and Hardy have ever made. It presents the inimitable funsters in a typical Laurel and Hardy story replete with gags and fast and furious action.

LAUREL'S DAD WATCHES HIM MAKE COMEDY

Probably the most interested spectator on the Laurel and Hardy set at the Hal Roach studios during the filming of the stellar duo's most recent comedy short, "Thicker Than Water," was an aged English gentleman, Arthur Jefferson. For hours at a time he would sit in rapt attention watching the filming of the picture, occasionally offering a comment in subdued tones to his wife, who accompanied him. It was quite apparent that the spectator, who was in his middle seventies, had more than a casual interest in the proceedings.

Mr. Jefferson, father of Stan Laurel, whose true name is Stanley Jefferson, was enjoying his first visit to America and his initial experience in an American motion picture studio. He came over from London especially to spend a few months with his "boy," of whom he is extremely proud. It was the first time he had ever seen his famous son work in pictures.

Noted Actor Himself

One of the last of the old school of English actors, Mr. Jefferson, during his long career in British theatricals has also served the profession as a producer, impresario and as a theatre manager. Throughout his entire life he has been devoted to the stage and it was his supreme hope that Stanley would follow in his footsteps. But never in his fondest dreams did his mind conjure the picture of eminence and fame that was to come to his boy.

Everyone on the set got a great "kick" out of the enthusiasm the old gentleman displayed. He was interested in the cameras and the other mechanical paraphernalia common to all studios as well as the work of the actors. Nothing escaped his eyes and his questions were those of one who possessed a keen sense and knowledge of theatrical in general.

"Thicker Than Water" is the last two-reeler to be made by Laurel and Hardy under the Hal Roach-M-G-M banner. In the future the stellar comedy team will be starred in four-reel and full-length productions. This is in answer to public demand, according to Hal Roach, who first brought Stan and Ollie together seven years ago.

Stan Laurel Admits He Hates to Wipe Dishes!

Nearly every one has a pet aversion. Stan Laurel's is wiping dishes, for as a child he was called upon to perform this rite nightly for years. So when a scene in "Thicker Than Water," the latest Laurel and Hardy comedy short, made it necessary for him to dry dishes as Ollie Hardy washed them, Stan did not relish the duty but reluctantly complied with the director's orders for art's sake.

His only satisfaction was in seeing the crockery destroyed before the scene was completed. "Thicker Than Water," a Hal Roach-M-G-M fun film, which comes to the . . . . Theatre next . . . ., is the last two-reeler the stellar comics will make. In the future they will appear in four-reel and feature length productions exclusively.

Stars and Director Called Mirth's Three Musketeers

Stan Laurel, Oliver Hardy and James Horne, director, might well be termed "The Three Musketeers of Mirth."

It is indeed a fitting sobriquet for the trio of comedy-minded fellows who are largely responsible for the hilarious two-reel fun film, "Thicker Than Water," which comes to the . . . . Theatre next . . . . For throughout the past decade, at various times, this combination has given the screen a number of its most humorous entertainments, including, among others, the recent Laurel and Hardy full-length feature, "Bonnie Scotland," and several years prior, "Beau Hunks."

The secret of their successful triumvirate may be attributed to their ability to work together "hand in glove." The trio creates a jovial atmosphere in which all workers expend their best efforts to make the picture a successful one. The three are also the merriest of friends and their clever repartee between scenes is often the inspiration for new gags or situations in the comedies.

Each one is a veteran at entertainment. Stan Laurel was reared in a theatrical atmosphere and has done no work other than furnishing laughs for audiences. Oliver Hardy, although trained in the legal profession, participated in stage presentations even during his high school days. Jimmy Horne, like Laurel, was reared in a theatrical atmosphere. He became a motion picture director in 1911 with the old Kalem Company. And all three have specialized in comedy.

On the Hal Roach "lot" everyone knows there's something very merry in the air when Stan, Ollie and Jimmy are seen in a huddle. For that reason they have become known there, at least, as "The Three Musketeers of Mirth."

Country of Origin, U. S. A.

Her First Acting Job Paid 25 Cents a Week!

Daphne Pollard, who essays the feminine character lead in the new Laurel and Hardy fun opus, "Thicker Than Water," coming to the . . . . Theatre next . . . ., received a salary of twenty-five cents a week as a child actress with the Australian theatrical troupe, "The Pollards," which toured this country for several years with great success. Incidentally, Daphne is not related to the Pollard who owned and managed the company which bore that name.

To earn this insignificant sum, the child player was called upon to sell song books during the intermission of the plays in which she had a prominent part. The diminutive actress is seen as Hardy's nagging wife in "Thicker Than Water," a Hal Roach-M-G-M comedy short.

NOTE:

In all advertising and publicity you issue in conjunction with the showing of "Thicker Than Water," bear down on the fact that this is the last opportunity to see Laurel and Hardy in a two-reel picture. As you undoubtedly know, in the future the stellar funsters will appear in four-reelers and full feature length comedies only.

CHEERS FROM THE CRITICS

"Best proof in the world that the team of Stan Laurel and Oliver Hardy should never be separated is provided in this knockout comedy. As an example of perfect comedy teamwork as well as in its results as amusement, it takes front rank. Plenty of swell comedy gags are sprinkled throughout."

—THE FILM DAILY

"Laurel and Hardy return here with most of their old tricks, but they do have several new ones that should have audiences holding their sides. During the last few feet of the film they reach new comedy heights. With Hardy the henpecked husband of Daphne Pollard and Laurel their boarder, the way is opened for the two comics to do their stuff and they take every advantage of the opportunities offered. Miss Pollard and James Finlayson are capable foils for the two comedians and hold their own for the most part when competing with them for laughs. One of the funniest shorts Laurel and Hardy have turned out in some time and one to be recommended anywhere."

—MOTION PICTURE DAILY

For Your Front! For the Kids! Laurel and Hardy Masks!

In advance . . . use these ticket-selling masks in your inner lobby . . . mount them at either end of a banner card. For the showing . . . string them from your canopy . . . with an outside distribution to the kids.

The mask consists of a life-size reproduction of Laurel or Hardy, and is held in place by means of rubber bands.

Prices: 500, $11; 5,000 at $20 per thousand; 10,000 at $18.75 per thousand; 25,000 at $18 per thousand; 50,000 at $16 per thousand; 50,000 and over at $15 per thousand. For further details write Einson-Freeman Co., Long Island City, New York.

LOBBY BALLYHOO

As a grandfather's clock plays an important part in several scenes in "Thicker Than Water," a suggestion for an appropriate contest, which ties in with the picture, follows: Offer a prize to the person who can guess nearest the time of day a grandfather's clock, placed in a conspicuous place in the theatre lobby, will run down.

NEWSPAPER CONTEST

In conjunction with your local newspaper conduct a contest to determine WHO SHOULD BE BOSS IN THE HOME—HUSBAND OR WIFE? Offer prizes for the best brief entries on this subject and have the newspaper publish the most logical essays. Of course, you will tie-in the fact that this age-old controversy is the basis for the Laurel and Hardy fun film, "THICKER THAN WATER."

TEASER THROWAWAY

A few days prior to the opening of this Laurel and Hardy fun film, distribute a quantity of small bottles or vials filled with a harmless fluid that resembles blood throughout town. Tie or paste a label to the receptacle with the following text: "WARNING! Stay away from the . . . . Theatre next . . . . night if you have high blood-pressure. Otherwise, you may laugh yourself to death! Blood is THICKER THAN WATER so Beware!"

TEASER

Three or four days prior to opening of "Thicker Than Water" have blotches of paint daubed on the streets, sidewalks and plate glass windows of vacant stores. The color should be a vivid red or scarlet to resemble blood but should be easily removable to avoid complications with the authorities. The opening day of the picture, letter in white over the red blotches, "See Laurel and Hardy in 'Thicker Than Water' at the . . . . Theatre." This inexpensive teaser campaign should cause a lot of comment and attract attention.

LOBBY CUTOUT

The three-sheet cutout reproduced above is available at your exchange as a three-sheet. It is suggested that the exhibitor mount this three-sheet on compo board and make his own individual cutout.

CATCHLINES

There's Heaps of Whoopee and Oodles of Laughs in This One!

When Stan Moves in on Ollie and His Bride Love Flies Out the Window!

America's Most Popular Screen Funsters Reach a New High in Hilarity!

In Which Deferred Payments and a Star-Boarder Spell Trouble for Mr. Hardy!

If You've Ever Bought Something on the Installment Plan Don't Miss This One!

Stan and Ollie Themselves Again —Just a Couple of Short Enders Trying to Get Along!

Ollie and His Bride Enjoy Love in a Cottage with Heaps of Fun on the Installment Plan!

Merrily They Roll Along Gathering No Moss but Leaving a Trail of Giggles and Guffaws!

You'll Laugh as You've Never Laughed Before When You See Stan and Ollie Cavort Through This One!

Stan a Star-Boarder — Ollie a Blushing Benedict—It's Great Fun for Everyone from Start to Finish!

Stan Helps Ollie Find Domestic Tranquility Only to Have It Knocked Down to a Higher Bidder in Love's Auction!

SHORT SHORTS

"Thicker Than Water," the Laurel and Hardy comedy currently showing at the .... Theatre, is the last two-reel comedy in which the famous funsters will appear. In the future, they will star in four-reel and full-length features only, according to Producer Hal Roach.

So much did the interior sets used as a background for the antics of Laurel and Hardy in their new fun short, "Thicker Than Water," appeal to a California college professor who visited the Hal Roach Studios while the picture was being filmed, that he asked permission to copy the plans for a new home he was about to build. The picture is now playing at the .... Theatre.

James (Jimmy) Horne, who directed Laurel and Hardy in their latest two-reel fun film, "Thicker Than Water," currently showing at the .... Theatre, also wielded the megaphone for the full-length feature production in which the comedy duo are starred, "Bonnie Scotland." Horne has several other pictures with Stan and Ollie to his credit, notably "Beau Hunks," one of their highly successful earlier comedies.

MANNERISM CONTEST

Here's an amusing contest or the youngsters to be held on the stage on the first or the last night of the showing of "Thicker Than Water." Offer prizes for the best imitators of the screen mannerisms of either Stan Laurel or Oliver Hardy.

For example, the former is especially remembered for the way he scratches his head in a perplexed manner and for his cry-baby tactics. Ollie is trademarked by his coyness and by his tie-flicking propensity.

It need not be essential that the kids make up or costume themselves in the manner of the two comics. The awards should be made solely on the children's ability to imitate Laurel or Hardy's individual mannerisms.

TEASER

Three or four days prior to opening of "Thicker Than Water" have blotches of paint daubed on the streets, sidewalks and plate glass windows of vacant stores. The color should be a vivid red or scarlet to resemble blood but should be easily removable to avoid complications with the authorities. The opening day of the picture, letter in white over the red blotches, "See Laurel and Hardy in 'Thicker Than Water' at the .... Theatre." This inexpensive teaser campaign should cause a lot of comment and attract attention.

AD MATS

Newspaper Ad Mats Free!
At Your M-G-M Exchange

POSTERS

Original one sheet for "Thicker Than Water"

EIGHT 11 x 14 LOBBY DISPLAYS!

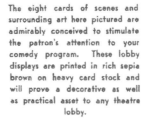

The eight cards of scenes and surrounding art here pictured are admirably conceived to stimulate the patron's attention to your comedy program. These lobby displays are printed in rich sepia brown on heavy card stock and will prove a decorative as well as practical asset to any theatre lobby.

"Thicker Than Water" before..........

......and after!

HAL ROACH presents

STAN LAUREL

OLIVER HARDY

BEAU HUNKS

COUNTY HOSPITAL

PERFECT DAY

BLOTTO

After the release of "Thicker Than Water" the demand for Laurel and Hardy shorts was still high. To fill in the void, four films from 1929 - 1932 were reissued.

EXPLOITATION

SELL LIKE FEATURE In Laurel and Hardy you have two marquee names that are favorites with every type of audience. Smart showmen will take full advantage of their box-office importance by giving their pictures feature prominence in all publicity, ads and lobby displays. One-sheet posters, ad mats and 8x10 stills are available at your M-G-M Exchange.

FIND LOCAL DOUBLES A stunt of proven effectiveness is a search to find local doubles for Laurel and Hardy. This can be conducted as a contest by either newspaper or radio station. Another version of this stunt is an offer to admit gratis fifty or so kids who parade to your theatre costumed and made-up to resemble either of the comedians.

PAPIER MACHE HEADS For street ballyhoo, lobby and window displays and innumerable other purposes the Laurel and Hardy papier mache masks are a worthwhile investment. Measuring 30 inches high, 20 inches wide and 9 inches deep, and finished in natural colors, these masks can be ordered direct from R. Fiore, 72 Thomas St., New York City. Price is $16 for set of two.

"SOURPUSS" SCREENING Get your newspaper to work with you on a screening for "sourpusses" which can be set up as a promotion stunt for their classified section. Thru their want-ads announce that six of the town's worst dead-pans will be chosen to view your Laurel-Hardy picture, with $5 awarded to any of those who can sit thru the screening without laughing. Photos of these sourpusses can be used in promotion ads as compelling evidence that their want-ads can produce any desired result.

NEWSBOYS DERBY The derby hat which is always the headpiece worn by the comedy pair, suggests a simple and effective ballyhoo stunt for your Laurel and Hardy pictures. From larger hat stores you can purchase a quantity of derbies from their old stock shelves for as little as five or ten cents apiece. Let your artists letter Laurel and Hardy and your theatre name on the crown. Pass them out to newsboys on principal downtown corners with the understanding that if they wear them during your showing they will receive a free admission.

SNAP GLOOMY GUSSES An old standby and always good is the roving newspaper photographer who snaps people at random in the downtown section. Have the cameraman search daily for the gloomiest expressions, with guest tickets offered to all those photographed.

FREE AD MATS

BEAU HUNKS

Highlights

Life is sweet to Laurel and Hardy as Stan sits about home reading and Oliver sings and plays love ballads on the piano. Suddenly Oliver stops singing to show Stan an autographed picture from his "Jeanie Weenie" and tell of his love for the girl. As they talk a letter from the girl is delivered and Stan reads it to his love-sick pal only to discover that the girl is through and "in love with another." Oliver is heart-broken so the two of them join the Foreign Legion "to forget." After the preliminary routine of enlistment they retire to the barracks where they see about half the men with autographed pictures of "Jeanie." They go to the commanding officer to tell him they don't care to stay and discover that he too has a picture of the girl. The officer bawls them out and sends them immediately on a long hike on the desert. Upon returning dead-tired the men retire only to be ousted shortly for another desert trek to rescue a fort being attacked by Riffs. On their way to the fort the troup runs into a violent sand storm and Stan and Oliver are lost. They finally reach the besieged fort alone but just as they begin their military routine the Riffs close in. For protection Stan and Oliver run into a room in which several kegs of tacks are stored. A bare-footed Riff storms in after them but Stan throws some tack on the floor and the Riff steps on them. Seeing the effect of the tacks Stan and Oliver sprinkle thousands of them in the gateway of the fort. As the Riffs break in they step on the tacks in their bare feet and are all dancing about in pain when the reserve soldiers arrive. Stan and Oliver capture the Riff chieftain in the melee and when he is searched they find an autographed picture of "Jeanie Weenie" for a fade out.

Director Turns Actor

When is a movie director not a director?

When he's an actor!

This answer would hardly place one at the head of the class but such was the position in which James Horne found himself during the filming of "Beau Hunks," the latest Laurel and Hardy Hal Roach comedy now playing at the .... Theatre. Not only did he essay the role of an actor, he also took orders from actors.

It all came about while filming night scenes for the picture. A small but important part was open in which some ambitious actor might score individual honors as a chieftain of Arabian Riffs. Three different players were rehearsed for the part but none of them came up to the expectations of director Horne.

It was too late at night to get another actor to the studio for the part so with grim determination Horne donned a Riff chieftain's attire, plastered some hirsute adornment over his face and took his position before the camera. Action of the scene forced Horne to take orders from Laurel and Hardy, who, as liegionnaires, held him captive.

FUN IS NOT FUN

It's not always fun being funny. Laurel and Hardy testified to this while filming "Beau Hunks," their latest Hal Roach-MGM comedy which comes........ to the .... Theatre. For several days these two comedians drilled and tramped under a sizzling California sun with the temperature tickling 100 degrees dressed in heavy woolen uniforms of the Foreign Legion and packing full military packs on their backs. On top of this they spent two days in a movie produced sand storm.

Catchlines

Four Reels Of Furious Fun!

•

One Long Loud Laugh!

•

They're In The Foreign Legion Now!

•

They Took To The Desert To Forget The Gal Who Deserted Them!

•

SIT DOWN IN THE DESERT . . . When The Boys Put Tacks Under Their Bare Feet The Riffs Couldn't Stand It!

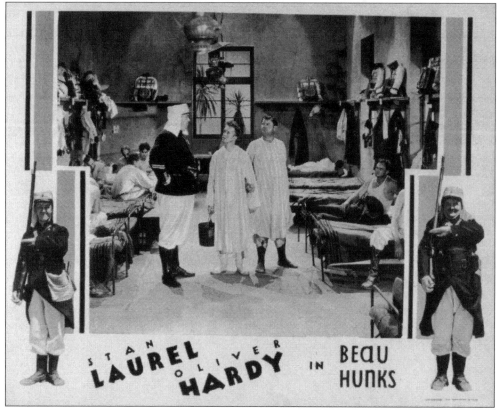

STAN LAUREL OLIVER HARDY IN BEAU HUNKS

STAN LAUREL OLIVER HARDY IN BEAU HUNKS

 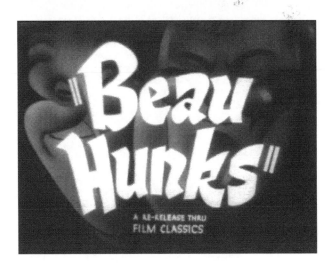

BLOTTO

Highlights

Messrs. Laurel and Hardy would very much like to go out for an evening of whoopee, but there's one little thing that is keeping Laurel from joining his friend Hardy. That one little thing is Mrs. Laurel (successor to Sherlock Holmes). Mrs. Laurel absolutely refuses to let her beloved husband go out, unless, of course, it is on a matter of important business.

Mr. Hardy calls Mr. Laurel on the telephone and urges him to send a telegram to himself, calling him away for the evening on said important business. Unfortunately Mrs. Laurel is listening in on the conversation, thereby getting the "low-down" on the plot. When she hears that they are going to snitch her bottle of pre-war (pre-the-next-war) liquor, she rushes downstairs, empties out the real stuff and substitutes it with cold tea, pepper, horse-radish, mustard, Perrin Sauce and salt. In the meanwhile Stan writes himself a telegram, takes it outside and rings the bell. He rushes inside again, answers the bell and gets his telegram from an imaginary Western Union Boy. Mrs. Laurel is so sorry Mr. Laurel has to go out, but nevertheless gets his hat and kisses him goodbye. Mr. Laurel joins Mr. Hardy and off they go to the opening of the Rainbow Night Club.

At the night club, Mr. Hardy has much difficulty in getting the first drink down, but Mr. Laurel drinks his without a murmur and likes it. After a series of complicated situations, Stan thinks of his wife's dismay at discovering her liquor all gone and gets a laughing jag. He tells Oliver about it, and they both roar with laughter. Even the sight of Mrs. Laurel, sitting in a booth behind them, doesn't stop them. That is, until she tells them they have been drinking cold tea. Sobering up immediately, they dash out of the club and climb into a cab. Mrs. Laurel follows with a thirty caliber rifle and just as the cab is about a half block away, takes a shot at it. The cab falls all to pieces and Laurel and Hardy fall out.

Its In The Mind!

The smartest cocktail of the season has nothing on the drinks that Mrs. Laurel mixes in "Blotto," the latest Hal Roach-MGM comedy which is on the program tonight at the .... Theatre. Laurel and Hardy think it is the real stuff, and imagine they get drunk from the results of it. Only when Mrs. Laurel tells them it is nothing but cold tea do they sober up.

ICED TEA JUG

The theme song of "Blotto," Laurel and Hardy's latest Hal Roach-MGM comedy, which is now on the program at the .... Theatre, is "The Curse Of An Aching Heart." Oliver Hardy's whiskey tenor would make a confirmed drunkard tear at his hair with envy and Stan Laurel's ditto alto would be the pride of a Limehouse rummy. And the wonder is, they do it all on iced tea!

Three Times—And Out

Laurel and Hardy got blotto (meaning drunk in the King's English) in three languages. That is, they went through the scenes of "Blotto," their latest Hal Roach-MGM comedy, now on the program at the .... Theatre, three times; once for the English version, once for the French and once for the Spanish. This was the first Roach comedy to be made with a French version, as well as English and Spanish.

Catchlines

Extra Length — Extra Laugh Special!

•

TEE-HEE . . . Stan And Oliver Get Drunk On Iced Tea!

•

They Laughed When The Boys Sat Down To Drink — And So Will You!

•

The Boys Were Whooping It Up — Until Their Iced Tea Let Them Down!

•

Stan And Oliver Step Out For A Rendezvous But Friend Wife Is A Step Ahead Of Them!

"Blotto" was filmed in three languages, English, Spanish (La Vida Nocturna), and French (Une Nuit Extravagante). The photo above shows the wives from each version. From left to right: Anita Garvin, Linda Loredo, and Georgette Rhodes. In the following photos the studio picture number is on the lower right. Photos where the number is followed by the letters "FR" are from the French version.

Stan Laurel and Georgette Rhodes relaxing at home (FR).

Georgette Rhodes speaks to Oliver Hardy on the phone while Stan Laurel waits for her reaction (FR).

Oliver Hardy, Tiny Sanford, and Stan Laurel (FR).

Oliver Hardy, Baldwin Cooke, and Stan Laurel (FR).

Oliver Hardy and Stan Laurel enjoy the floorshow in "Blotto" (FR).

Oliver Hardy and Stan Laurel get "Blotto" (FR).

Oliver Hardy, Stan Laurel and Georgette Rhodes (FR).

Highlights

Oliver is in the hospital with a broken leg and Stan calls upon him with a gift of hard-boiled eggs and nuts. Stan tries to crack a nut with the weight which keeps Oliver's leg suspended in air. As he lifts the weight Oliver's leg drops and hits the doctor on the head which so enrages him that he tries to take the weight from Stan but falls out the window, saving himself from falling to the pavement below by hanging onto the weight. Stan eventually gets him inside the room again and the doctor immediately orders them both out of the hospital.

Stan sits on a chair on which a nurse had laid a large hypodermic needle filled with sleeping fluid. When they finally get downstairs and into their open flivver Stan starts nodding and dozing.

After many narrow escapes they finally land between two street cars. There is a loud crash and an officer tells them to move over to the side of the street. The car, however, is bent in the middle so that the front wheels will turn only in one direction, causing them to go around in circles, and the officer proceeds to write out their ticket.

Catchlines

Oliver's Broken Leg Gave Stan A Pain In The Neck!

●

Oliver Went To The Hospital To Recuperate But The Doctor's Couldn't!

●

Oliver Was Feeling Swell — Until Stan Took Him Out Of The Hospital!

●

Oliver Was Ill — But It Was Stan Who Suffered!

Making Laffs No Fun For Comedians

The business of making movie audiences laugh is no laughing matter to Laurel and Hardy.

During the filming of "County Hospital," the Hal Roach-MGM comedy now playing at the .... Theatre, Oliver Hardy hung suspended by one leg with his head down for approximately one hour. Of course, he did not hang the full hour at one time as the scene was photographed several times before the desired effect was obtained.

In this particular scene Hardy was drawn up by a leg incased in a huge plaster cast, supposedly a broken leg. The comedian was lying in a hospital bed and his partner Stan Laurel accidentally dropped the weight out of the window causing Hardy's sudden ascension.

Considering the comedian's weight the "gag" in itself was a big undertaking. The greatest difficulty was experienced in getting the proper lighting on the star's face while he was suspended in the air as the blood would rush to his head and he would photograph very dark. After several experiments he used a vey light make-up which photographed natural.

HERE'S HOW FUN FILM WAS BORN

That old wheeze "did you ever hear about my operation" served as inspiration to Laurel and Hardy for the writing of "County Hospital," their latest Hal Roach-MGM comedy which comes .... to the .... Theatre.

The comedians were enjoying an evening of recreation together at one of the popular Beverly Hills clubs. During a session of cards someone at the table, in an effort to break the tenseness of the game, pulled the old bromide about their operation. It got a laugh and also started to work the imaginative minds of the two comedians.

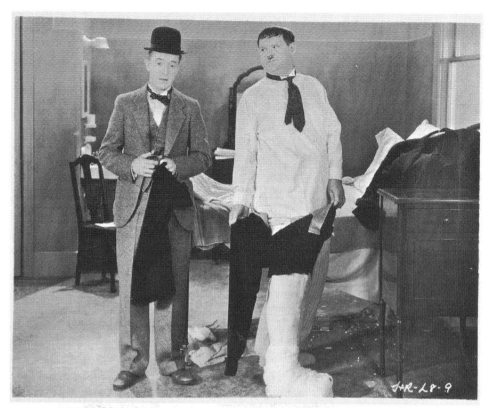

STAN LAUREL and OLIVER HARDY

STAN LAUREL and OLIVER HARDY

Highlights

A'picnicking would go Mr. and Mrs. Laurel, Mr. and Mrs. Hardy and gouty Uncle Edgar on a lovely Sabbath morn. Stan and Oliver make the sandwiches, while the wives pack the lunch box. But Stan slips with the loaded tray, the sandwiches meet a messy end and the fight is on. When Sabbath peace reigns once more, the five holiday-seekers embark in their trusty Ford. But a treacherous nail lies in their path, and one of the rear tires slowly flattens. In the mix-up of changing tires, the intelligent Stan returns the original flat to the wheel's frame. The jack, hurled in anger by the disgusted Oliver, misses its target, Stan's head, and crashes through a near-by window. The entire neighborhood joins in the fray which follows. When quiet is restored and once more the five pic-nickers have taken their places in the car, the engine refuses to start. Oliver, cranking, asks Stan to throw out the clutch. Stan obeys him, and again the Sabbath quiet is shattered by the the sound of battle. In the heat of the turmoil, Oliver throws Stan against the hood of the car, and the engine starts. Waving good-bye to the assem-bled neighborhood, the five start jaunt-ily upon their excursion. Heads turned in last triumphant farewells, they fail to see the unpaved street and the yawning mudhole before them. The perfect day ends with a final plunge beneath muddy waters.

MOVIE MUD BATH

A huge mudhole was excavated and filled with water in one of the Hal Roach studio streets for the laugh-finale of Laurel and Hardy's comedy "Perfect Day," coming .... to the .... Theatre.

As two men of family who start out for a Sunday picnic, the comedians end their perfect day with a final plunge beneath the muddy waters. Only their famous derbies are left floating on the water as Laurel and Hardy, their wives, Uncle Edgar and their car all sink be-neath the surface.

The mudhole, eight feet deep, twenty feet long and twelve feet wide, was fitted with pulleys so that the automo-bile could be lowered to the bottom without accident. Isabelle Keith, Kay Deslys and Edgar Kennedy share the mudbath with Laurel and Hardy.

Laurel and Hardy Go A—Picnicking

Concerning the trials and tribulations of an average family on a picnic, the humor of Laurel and Hardy's newest funfilm, "Perfect Day," now playing at the .... Theatre, is based on its closeness to everyday experience.

Almost everyone, at some time or another in his life, has started forth on a holiday, only to meet with mis-hap and trouble. Spilled sandwiches, sore feet, punctured tires, stubborn automobile engines, quarrelling hus-bands and back-seat-driving wives are a part of everyone's experience.

In "Perfect Day," the two Hal Roach clowns, have built two reels of riotous fun around these universal happenings. Their perfect day of Sabbath picnick-ing starts with Stan's diastrous drop-ping of the sandwiches and ends with the final disappearance of the holiday-makers and their car beneath the waters of an unseen mudhole.

SMASH HIT

Fifty windows were smashed in one hilarious scene of the latest Laurel and ardy comedy, "Perfect Day," coming .... to the .... Theatre. The celebrated clown started a throwing match which involved an entire neigh-borhood, its windows and its windshelds.

Catchlines

Filmdom's Favorite Funsters!

●

A SMASH HIT — As Stan And Ollie Break Every Window In The Neigh-borhood!

●

GLOOM TAKES A HOLIDAY — As Stan And Ollie Set Out For A Pic-nic!

●

TODAY IS FUN-DAY . . . They Thought They Were Having A Pic-nic — Until Their Flivver Sank In A Mudhole!

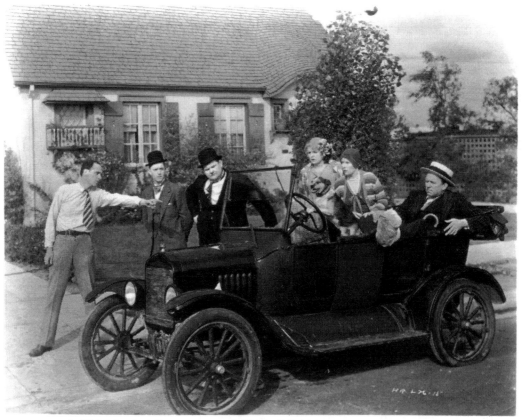

STAN LAUREL and OLIVER HARDY

"BERTH MARKS" PRESS SHEET

ALL TALKING COMEDY

HAL ROACH presents

STAN LAUREL AND OLIVER HARDY

in "BERTH MARKS"

Screen's Greatest Comedy Team
Riot of Laughs in Latest
Hal Roach--M-G-M Comedy

Released by
METRO-GOLDWYN-MAYER
1540 Broadway, New York, N. Y.
Any promotion suggestions or ideas should be sent to
HOWARD DIETZ
1540 Broadway, New York, N. Y.

Hal Roach — M-G-M Comedy
"Berth Marks"
Stars
Stan Laurel and
Oliver Hardy
Directed by
Lewis R. Foster
Photographed by
Len Powers
Film Editor
Richard Currier
Story Editor
H. M. Walker

STAN LAUREL *and* OLIVER HARDY *in* "BERTH MARKS"
A Hal Roach-MGM All Talking Comedy

STAN LAUREL *and* OLIVER HARDY
in "BERTH MARKS' — Hal Roach-
MGM All Talking Comedy

SCENE CUT NO. 3

SYNOPSIS

Stan and Oliver are vaudeville artists of the many-a-days. Stan has a cello. Oliver has a flowing coat and a vast managerial dignity. They meet at the station to catch a train for an engagement in far-off Pottsville. They find each other just as the locomotive is whistling out of the station. In gaining the steps of the last Pullman, they lose their music, their equilibrium, and their poise. After disturbing the peaceful slumber of the train's sleeping customers, they painfully attain the cramped privacy of their shared upper berth. But the night holds no rest for Stan and Oliver. With groans and heated argument they disrobe, tangling and untangling themselves, their clothes, and the furnishings of their sleeping quarters. They gain comfort and a reclining position just as the conductor calls, "Pottsville." The train pulls in and out, leaving them shivering in their underwear on the planks of the station platform. Their shoes and their cello depart with the speeding Pullman. After the train sprints the hapless Stan, is urged on to speed by the threatening rock in the hand of the irate Oliver. Unshod and unclothed, they disappear in the shadows of the grey dawn.

LAUREL AND HARDY'S "BERTH MARKS" IS FAST AND FURIOUS FUN IN A PULLMAN

A regulation size Pullman coach, complete in every detail was constructed on the sound stage of the Hal Roach studio for the hilarious train scenes of Laurel and Hardy's newest sound film, "Berth Marks," coming to the .... Theater......

Most of the riotous action of this two-reeler takes place in the cramped quarters of an upper berth, shared by the two fun-makers. As a setting for these scenes, the studio engineers built a standard size Pullman coach, equipped with regulation furnishings. The completed car had everything except the wheels.

In this reproduction to Mr. Pullman's contribution to the comfort of the traveling public, the Hal Roach - Metro-Goldwyn-Mayer comedy pair enacts the funniest and fastest scenes of its screen career. They set a new mark for comedy capers in "Berth Marks," their second experience before the microphones.

Lewis, R. Foster, who directed the pantomime of the silent films, is responsible for many of the laughs and smooth speed of their initial talkies. The dialogue is funny, but the action is funnier. One laugh follows another with breath-taking speed. The hilarity waxes fast and furious from opening shot to smashing finale.

Once more the screen's dizziest dumbells have rung the comedy bell, this time louder and longer than ever before.

Short Paragraphs

Stan Laurel and Oliver Hardy carry the laugh burden of their newest Hal Roach — M-G-M comedy, "Berth Marks," now playing at the ..... Theatre, without masculine or feminine aid or support. With the exception of a few extras to serve as a background, the comedy pair plays alone in its newest all-talking mirthfest.

* * *

Laurel and Hardy blaze a new trail of hilarity in their latest laugh-maker, "Berth Marks," coming to the ..... Theatre. As two wandering actors of the many-a-day vaudeville route they set a mad and merry pace in their newest talkfilm.

* * *

One long laugh is "Berth Marks," the latest spasm of the Hal Roach— Metro - Goldwyn - Mayer comedy clowns, Stan Laurel and Oliver Hardy, coming to the ..... Theatre ....

* * *

A story without a heroine, a comedy without a blonde, is Laurel and Hardy's latest Hal Roach — M-G-M mirth fest, "Berth Marks," at the ..... Theatre. Stan and Oliver have no time for women in the speedy action of their fastest and funniest all-talking farce.

* * *

Laurel and Hardy's newest funfilm, "Berth Marks," coming .... to the ..... Theatre will leave you black and blue with laughter. As two travelling vaudeville artists in an upper berth, they touch the high spots of comedy capers in this latest Hal Roach — M-G-M mirthfest.

* * *

Laurel and Hardy are coming to the ..... Theatre ..... in their brand new talkfilm, "Berth Marks." Watch them catch a train in a shower of sheet music, cellos, baggage and people. See their painful climb into their joint upper berth. Listen to them groan in the agony of their crowded disrobing. Laugh with them as they stand, forlorn and unclothed, in the dismal dawn of a dreary railroad station.

* * *

Slapstick comedy supreme is Laurel and Hardy's latest offering to the laughter - loving world, "Berth Marks" at the ..... Theatre. They use all the old tricks plus a bagful of new ones in this merry gloom-chaser from the Hal Roach—M-G-M studios.

* * *

The entire world is laughing with the antics of the master slapstick artists, Stan Laurel and Oliver Hardy, in their masterpiece of clowning buffoonery, "Berth Marks," at the .... Theatre. Again the Hal Roach — M-G-M fun-makers ring the comedy bell in this all-talking funfilm.

* * *

"Berth Marks," the newest Laurel and Hardy comedy now playing at the ..... Theatre, has everything, voices, action, sound, thrills, laughter, Stan and Oliver. Don't miss it.

* * *

A new mark of laughter is left upon the world by "Berth Marks," the fastest and funniest Hal Roach— M-G-M talkfilm, starring the master funsters, Stan Laurel and Oliver Hardy.

* * *

Opening with a bang and closing with a smash, "Berth Marks," the newest Laurel and Hardy all-talking cyclone, is having audiences at the ..... Theatre gasping for breath. The screen's dizziest clowns talk, groan and make merry in their gayest Hal Roach — M-G-M mirthfest.

* * *

A merry melee of sound an daction is "Berth Marks," the newest Hal Roach — M-G-M all-talking laughfilm, starring the inimitable Stan Laurel and Oliver Hardy, coming to the ..... Theatre .... They are themselves, at their funniest best in their speediest film.

CATCHLINES

Fast and furious fun in a Pullman car is Laurel and Hardy's newest talkfilm "Berth Marks" at the ..... Theater.

See, hear, and suffer with Laurel and Hardy in the hilarious pain of their newest fan offering "Berth Marks" coming to the ..... Theater.

FAST FUN OF "BERTH MARKS" BASED ON REAL EXPERIENCE

The germ of the story idea for the merry-making of the newest Hal Roach - Metro-Goldwyn-Mayer talkfilm, "Berth Marks, staring comedy team, Laurel and Hardy which is now playing at the ..... Theater, was gained from similar experiences in the life of Stan Laurel.

Before starting his screen career the versatile Mr. Laurel spent many years trouping his native England, the Continent, and the United States with vaudeville and variety shows. With Charlie Chaplin, Stan was a member of Fred Karno's London Comedians, which came to America in 1910 to present its classic act, "A Night In An English Music Hall."

Many times during his long and varied traveling career Stan suffered the trials and tribulations endured by the two vaudevillians in "Berth Marks." His memory of the days of crowded journeys in narrow upper berths formed the basis of this laugh fest of a night in a Pullman Car.

In "Berth Marks," Laurel and Hardy play two traveling artists of the vaudeville stage. Most of the action of this fast and funny fable takes place in an upper berth of a sleeping coach. The noises of the speeding train add a new note of laughter to the riotous speech and actions of the two comedians.

"Berth Marks" is the second talking picture which has been made by the duet of funsters.

CATCHLINES

The screen's dizziest clowns in their speediest spasm, Laurel and Hardy in "Berth Marks" at the ..... Theater.

Two riotous reels of fun and voices in Laurel and Hardy's "Berth Marks," coming to the ..... Theater.

A mad and merry melee of mirth in Laurel and Hardy's newest talkfilm "Berth Marks," at the ..... Theater.

Comedy capers plus smashing sound make Laurel and Hardy's "Berth Marks," at the ..... Theater, the merriest mirthfest.

Hal Roach plus M-G-M plus the all-talking screen now give you comedies that draw like feature pictures at the box office. What an opportunity for live-wire showmen to emphasize the value of their attractions than never before. This particular comedy, and other Hal Roach - M-G-M all-talking comedies, are worthy of the same attention that you would give to a feature picture. And in this press sheet you will find everything you need to build a campaign on "Berth Marks" that will pay for itself many times over.

Everybody knows Laurel and Hardy and watches for their comedies. Newspaper advertising is a great bet for you - use the ad cuts available at your M-G-M exchange.

Even the paper on this comedy brings a laugh - and furthermore, it can't be missed. A few ones and threes scattered in good spots in your vicinity will have extra patronage waiting for your doors to open.

Put "Laurel and Hardy in All-Talking Comedy" in your marquee lights. Folks are watching for these boys, now!

The 11 x 14 lobby displays and the 8 x 10 black and white scene stills available at your M-G-M Exchange are great aids at dressing a lobby - especially when you are playing Laurel and Hardy. Prepare a large lobby announcement of this all-talking comedy using in conjunction with either of these two accessories.

Give the motion picture column of your local newspapers something to work with. Press stories and scenes from this picture are included in this press sheet. Most exhibitors get extra space with them regularly. You can do the same.

Even the
P A P E R
Brings a Laugh
and Brings Them In!

ACCESSORIES
AVAILABLE
ON THIS
PRODUCTION

Press Sheet
Subject 1 Sheet
8—11x14 Lobby Cards
Subject Slide
2—1 Col. Ad Mats
1—2 Col. Ad Mat
2—1 Col. Scene Mats
1—2 Col. Scene Mat

ORDER FROM YOUR
LOCAL EXCHANGE

A set of eight 11 x 14 lobby cards packed with all the action and humor of "Berth Marks." Use them for a display as suggested for your lobby or theatre front. Order from your local exchange.

STAN LAUREL *and* OLIVER HARDY *in* "BERTH MARKS"
A Hal Roach-MGM All Talking Comedy

STAN LAUREL *and* OLIVER HARDY *in* "BERTH MARKS"
A Hal Roach-MGM All Talking Comedy

STAN LAUREL *and* OLIVER HARDY *in* "BERTH MARKS"
A Hal Roach-MGM All Talking Comedy

STAN LAUREL *and* OLIVER HARDY *in* "BERTH MARKS"
A Hal Roach-MGM All Talking Comedy

STAN LAUREL *and* OLIVER HARDY *in* "BERTH MARKS"
A Hal Roach-MGM All Talking Comedy

STAN LAUREL *and* OLIVER HARDY *in* "BERTH MARKS"
A Hal Roach·MGM All Talking Comedy

STAN LAUREL *and* OLIVER HARDY *in* "BERTH MARKS"
A Hal Roach·MGM All Talking Comedy

PRESS SHEET
HAL ROACH - Metro-Goldwyn-Mayer
STAN LAUREL
AND
OLIVER HARDY
COMEDIES

Comedies That Pull Like Feature Pictures!   The Greatest
of All Comedy Teams Will Mean Plenty at the
B.O. if You Get Behind—

COME CLEAN

M·G·M COMEDY SPECIALS

A Hal Roach — M-G-M
Laurel and Hardy Comedy
"COME CLEAN"
Starring
Laurel and Hardy
Director
James W. Horne
Cameraman
Art Lloyd
Sound Engineer
Elmer Raguse
Story Editor
H. M. Walker
Film Editor
Richard Currier
A Victor Recording
Western Electric System
Running Time — 21 Minutes
Footage — 1880 Feet

IT COULD HAVE HAP-PENED TO ANYONE!

That's why Laurel & Hardy's "Come Clean" Is Rare Comedy Treat

All Laurel and Hardy comedies are laugh successes because these boys seem to have the capacity to extract fun from the most everyday things in life. Laughter is spontaneous throughout any one of their comedies because of their famed Laurel and Hardy manner. To bump one's nose is maddening, but to bump one's nose in the Laurel and Hardy way is quite laughable.

The comedians' latest Hal Roach comedy, "COME CLEAN", whch is now showing at the ..... Theatre, is a series of laugh enticing escapades. Mr. Laurel is funny, screamingly funny, when he writes a note to Mr. Hardy, telling him he called. Mr. Hardy is doubly funny in the receiving of the note. They are both a howling success in the purchase of a quart of ice cream, and when they try to hide a woman from their wives —well, if you don't enjoy Laurel and Hardy you have no sense of humor.

"COME CLEAN" is the pitiful story of two unexperienced men trying to hide a woman, a desperate woman, from their wives. The woman, a character of rather uncertain virtues, is portrayed by Mae Busch, and she certainly puts the comedians through their paces. As well as Miss Busch, Linda Loredo and Gertrude Astor have important parts as the respective wives of Laurel and Hardy.

James W. Horne directed this fun fest, with dialogue by H. M. Walker.

SYNOPSIS

The Hardys' anticipation of a nice quiet evening at home was shattered with the appearance of the Laurels, Mr. and Mrs. At the suggestion of Mr. Laurel the men go out for some ice cream, and on the way back encounter a woman with suicide in her mind. This desperate woman jumped over the parapet and into the swirling waters below. Mr. Hardy followed with the intentions of saving her. It was up to Mr. Laurel to save them both. The woman, who has a reward on her head, calls them both meddlesome fools because she didn't want to live, and therefore Messrs. Laurel and Hardy must take care of her. With no small amount of screaming they are finally compelled to take her up to Mr. Hardy's apartment, and hide her in the bedroom beyond the suspicious eyes of their wives. In the meanwhile detectives, having seen her enter, surround the apartment house. The wives discover the woman and Babe shoves her and Stan into the bathroom, absolving himself of all blame and committing Stan. The detectives, hearing the commotion, enter and break down the bathroom door. Stan is in the tub, a la ostrich style and the woman behind the door. The detectives capture the woman and tell Stan to appear at the station to collect the reward. Mr. Hardy is so mad that he pulls the stopper out of the bathtub and sends Mr. Laurel to the beach via the pipeline.

PUBLICITY

LAUREL-HARDY ABSURD? PERHAPS, BUT CERTAINLY FUNNY

"Come Clean", latest comedy, ranks high among their screen successes

Laurel and Hardy welcome absurd situations if only for the fact that they have to get out of them. After the usual exclamation of Mr. Hardy, "Here's another nice mess you've got me into", the boys proceed in their own bunglesome manner to absolve themselves.

In "COME CLEAN", which is now on the program at the ...... Theatre, Laurel and Hardy aimlessly wander from one ticklish "mess" to another. One often wonders how two men could be so dumb, so utterly brainless, and live, although both Mr. Laurel and Mr. Hardy claim that it took long years of study and practicing to appear as fatuous as they do on the screen.

"COME CLEAN" is the story of two men, their wives, and a desperate woman. Laurel and Hardy have the hard luck of rescuing a woman from the river and this woman rewards them by forcing herself on them regardless of their lives. The boys have a hard time keeping their little secret when the woman hides herself in the Hardy bedroom and the two wives converse in the room beyond.

Gertrude Astor and Linda Loredo play the boys' wives, and Mae Busch is the other woman. They are all good and there is no gainsaying the fact that for real laughs no comedians on the screen today can approach Stan Laurel and Oliver Hardy.

SHORT PARAGRAPHS

With the capable assistance of Gertrude Astor, Linda Loredo and Mae Busch, Stan Laurel and Oliver Hardy have produced two of the funniest and fastest reels in comedy history. "COME CLEAN", their latest Hal Roach comedy, which is now on the program at the ...... Theatre is another notch in the careers of these irresistible comedians.

＊ ＊ ＊

For an inexhaustible amount of fun and laughter Laurel and Hardy, famed Hal Roach comedians, can always be depended upon. Their latest fun fest, "COME CLEAN", which is now on the program at the ...... Theatre is the best bit of nonsense yet enacted by these popular comedians.

CATCHLINES

"COME CLEAN" which is now playing at the ...... Theatre, is the best bit of nonsense yet enacted by the popular Hal Roach comedians, Laurel and Hardy.

* * *

Beware of strange women is the moral of Laurel and Hardy's latest Hal Roach two reeler, "COME CLEAN", which is now on the program at the ...... Theatre.

* * *

Laurel and Hardy, crazier and dumber than ever, once more spot the .... Theatre program with their irresistible humor. Their latest Hal Roach offering is titled "COME CLEAN".

* * *

During these "repression days" a laugh is a fine tonic. Let Laurel and Hardy doctor you up with "COME CLEAN" at the .... Theatre tonight.

* * *

Laurel and Hardy .. in another fine mess. This one is titled "COME CLEAN" and is now showing at the ...... Theatre.

* * *

Mr. Hardy believes husbands should always tell the truth to their wives. Mr. Laurel is crazy too. And that's why Laurel and Hardy "COME CLEAN" at the .... Theatre tonight in their latest Hal Roach two reeler.

LAUREL AND HARDY IN COME CLEAN AT STATE

Surely See Latest Laugh Hit of Celebrated Comedy Team

"COME CLEAN" is the title of the newest Laurel and Hardy Hal Roach comedy, which is now showing at the .... Theatre, and "COME CLEAN" it is, for before the finale fade out of this comedy Mr. Laurel, Mr. Hardy and Miss Mae Busch all get good duckings. Mr. Hardy and Miss Busch chose the Hal Roach Studio pool for their bathing and Mr. Laurel did his cleansing in the bath-tub.

The Messrs. Laurel and Hardy happened upon a desperate woman about to commit suicide. She does and Mr. Hardy tries to save her but in doing so almost drowns himself. It takes Mr. Laurel to save them both. This ungrateful woman fastens herself on Messrs. Laurel and Hardy like a leech — she didn't want to live, but as long as the dumb-bells wanted to save her they have to take care of her.

The boys try to hide the woman from their wives, and Mr. Hardy, in one last attempt, shoves the woman and Stan into the bathroom. It is here that Stan fills the tub with water and hides in it a la ostrich style — ducking number three. If it takes clean people to make a clean comedy "COME CLEAN" is immaculate.

EASY EXPLOITATION BETS

Laurel and Hardy can be exploited as easy as a feature picture. They are known and looked for by every movie-goer. The complaint of the public is that exhibitors do not give them sufficient prominence in their program advertising.

The advertising and exploitation accessories provided on all Laurel and Hardy comedies should provide the backbone of your campaign. The six foot lobby cutout which has just been made available should be in every theatre playing the series. The cost per release comes to but one dollar for the black and white and one dollar and a quarter for the color cutout. Little enough when you figure the extra business that this stand will bring.

The black and white scene stills and the 11 x 14 display cards available at your M-G-M Exchange make possible the arrangement of window displays in stores dealing in kitchen equipment, bathroom fixtures and with soda fountains. A supplementary card or one sheet to be added in each instance announcing the showing of the picture at your theatre.

SHORT PARAGRAPHS

Laurel and Hardy, famous Hal Roach laugh enticers, will extract many of the giggles, most of the laughs and all of the howls of merriment from the audience of the .. .. Theatre where their latest comedy is showing tonight.

* * *

Although the odds are against Laurel and Hardy in "COME CLEAN", their latest Hal Roach rib-tickler which is now on the program at the ...... Theatre, they manage to worm their way out of the most complicated mess of their comedy careers. "COME CLEAN" is the story of two harassed gentlemen, Laurel and Hardy, their wives, Linda Loredo and Gertrude Astor, and a woman of rather uncertain virtues, Mae Busch.

* * *

LAUREL & HARDY PROVE THEIR COMEDY GENIUS

"Come Clean" an Example of Spontaneous Humor and Ingenuity

There are very few stars left who "shoot from the cuff" because of the complete story department every large studio carries. These departments, with their well known and famous writers, prepare the stories for the stars and when it is time for shooting a script complete in every detail is in existence. Scene by scene the picture follows the script in which all dialogue and action are enumerated.

With Laurel and Hardy, famous Hal Roach comedians, however, it is different. If time is short and they get the germ of an idea they prepare the barest outline of their script. Their powers of ad libbing and spontaneous fun eliminate long and lengthy stories, and too, their funniest moments seem to result from their impromptu acting before the camera.

For the story of "COME CLEAN", their latest comedy which is now on the program at the ...... Theatre. Laurel and Hardy decided to save a drowning woman who didn't want to be saved and therefore thrust herself upon them. The boys then had to hide the woman from their wives and figure out some way to get rid of her.

The script was very short, but with the comedians shooting from the cuff — adding more action with each scene shot — the desired amount of film was ready at the completion of the comedy. Laurel and Hardy know their own comedy capacity and act accordingly. Of course, they have many times used a script complete in every detail which they have followed scene by scene, but whether they have this finished story or not, all of their comedies so far have been pronounced laugh successes.

STAN LAUREL *and* OLIVER HARDY

One Col. Star Cut (Stock)

STAN LAUREL and OLIVER HARDY

8 - 11 x 14 LOBBY DISPLAYS

 Now Playing

POSTERS

—

SUBJECT 1 SHEET

Printed in U. S. A.

Full Color Portrait for Lobby Frame or Cut-out!

Below is a reproduction of a splendid oil painting, painted by a well-known portrait painter in life-like colors. Beautiful and striking — a splendid bid for extra patronage in your lobby or on your theatre front. For use in advance or during the showing of any of their releases. Full one sheet size — mounted on heavy board for use as cutout or in frame. Special processes make possible the extremely low price — $1.50 f.o.b. your M-G-M exchange. Every theatre should have at least two on hand.

STAN LAUREL and OLIVER HARDY

"BLOTTO" FOREIGN "FUN FARE" HERALD

WHITEWAY TRADERS
BRING TO YOU
LAUREL and HARDY FUNFARE
THE GREATEST LAUGH MOVIE FOR THE LONGEST, LOUDEST LAFFS YOU EVER HEARD.

Mr. Laurel & Mr. Hardy are preparing to go out on a picnic with their wives. While they are dressing in excitement there is a telephone call which is being attended by Mr. Hardy. He is invited with his friend for a party arranged in their honour. He thinks himself as a rock of Gibralter in his determination but he cannot resist the temptation. He wants to be big and signals his friend, who is unaware of his new plan. They want to be big in their own way but they cannot dis-please their wives. They hit upon many laugh provoking ideas and sensational ways of facing the most difficult situations so baffling to overcome. They bring to life the boy-hood days passed together that will make you roar. You will laugh and laugh to see the inimitable comedy stars in their most unusual laugh provoking situations. We bet you will enjoy to your utmost the hilarous comedy. It is the cent per cent entertainment for one and all.

The end.

Paper C. C. No. 47432.
Dt. 28th April 1950.
Length 10625 Ft.

(THE NICKEL NURSER——PRESS SHEET)

HAL ROACH presents

CHARLEY CHASE

PRESS SHEET

—what a run for their money the fans will get when they see—

THE NICKEL NURSER

A METRO-GOLDWYN-MAYER TALKING COMEDY

Gorgeous Creations Displayed in "Nickel Nurser"

Exquisite Fashions Enough to Make Parisian Designers Envious

Who said Paris was the style center of the world?

One look at the stunning creations worn by the beautiful girls supporting Charley Chase in "NICKEL NURSER," his latest Hal Roach-M-G-M comedy now playing at the .... Theatre, would make one think twice before committing themselves.

This drawing room farce is resplendent with gorgeous and fascinating new styles in women's wearing apparel from negligees to evening clothes. All the clothes worn by the girls were especially designed and modeled exclusively for use in this picture.

Six yards of metal cloth alone was used in creating an evening dress which was seen in only three scenes. Approximately twelve yards of satin, especially selected from imported materials, was required for the two evening gowns worn by Hazel Howell and Estelle Eterre.

A combination of fur, velvet and georgette was used in designing a flimsy creation in the form of a negligee. A pair of step-ins and a beautiful black lace negligee covering a pair of scanties of the same material were especially created for one of the girls. So well did she like the clothes that she asked to purchase them at the completion of the picture.

The supporting cast of "NICKEL NURSER" includes Thelma Todd, Billy Gilbert and the three blondes, Hazel Howell, Estelle Eterre and Geraldine D'vorak. Warren Doane directed the picture.

SHORT PARAGRAPHS

Three thousand yards of spaghetti was used with a liberal amount of cream sauce to drench Billy Gilbert, who essays the role of a butler in the latest Charley Chase-Hal Roach comedy, "NICKEL NURSER," now playing at the .... Theatre. After picking the stringy mess from his hair, eyes, ears and collar the actor gave thanks that it was not hot soup.

SYNOPSIS

Charley Chase in the role of an economist enters a millionaire's home in which three lovely girls are enjoying all the extravagances of modern youth. He comes into the home under the illusion the children are babies, but when he discovers they are eligible young ladies he finds himself confronted by a difficult situation. He endeavors to preach to them the crime of wasteful extravagance, but it does little good. Through a subterfuge he becomes enmeshed in complications with the servant girl, thinking she is one of three sisters he is hired to cure of spending so much money. He becomes engaged in a series of embarrassing and very uncomfortable situations which finally so enrages the butler, who is married to the servant girl, that open warfare is declared on Charley. After practically ruining the beautiful home Charley discovers his mistake and the hoax which has been played upon him and finds happiness in the arms of the prettiest girl.

"NICKEL NURSER"— RIOTOUS ROACH COMEDY AT STATE THEATRE

Charley Chase in Role of Economist Provides Endless Fun

Economy is the watchword of the world at present.

And it was economy that inspired Director Warren Doane and Charley Chase to write "NICKEL NURSER," the latest Hal Roach-M-G-M comedy now playing at the..............Theatre.

The extravagant expenditures of individuals as well as business houses and corporations prompted the idea of using economy for the main plot and theme of this rollicksome drawing-room farce. The penny-pinching methods of Charley Chase in the role of an economist in the household of a millionaire will excite laughter in the severest comedy critic.

Not only does the comedian aim to conserve on the family budget, but he endeavors to teach extravagant youth how to spend what little money they may have. When he allows love to mix with his work, however, the damage he is responsible for more than exceeds the few pennies he might have saved.

Thelma Todd appears opposite Charley Chase in "NICKEL NURSER" and adds much to the humor of the film. Billy Gilbert, a character comedian, and three beautiful blondes, namely, Hazel Howell, Estelle Eterre and Geraldine D'vorak, also appear to advantage. Warren Doane directed.

There's nothing like being a family man, providing one wishes to avoid the possible subterfuge of women. It was Charley Chase's ignorance in regards to such matters that made him mistake the hair protector and smock worn by Thelma Todd as the garb of a servant girl in "NICKEL NURSER," his latest Hal Roach M-G-M comedy now playing at the..............Theatre. And does he pay plenty for his ignorance.

An idea of extravagant youth may be gained from the latest Charley Chase-Hal Roach comedy," "NICKEL NURSER," now playing at the..............Theatre, in which a silky, lace-trimmed pair of step-ins are valued at $40.00. The step-ins, made of the sheerest imported silk, could be easily carried in the average sized women's coin purse.

CATCHLINES

Economy is all right, but you can't afford to miss Charley Chase in "NICKEL NURSER," his latest Hal Roach-M-G-M comedy.

There's no economy in missing Charley Chase in "NICKEL NURSER," his latest Hal Roach-M-G-M comedy.

It's all right to pinch pennies, but spend a few nickels to see Charley Chase in "NICKEL NURSER," a Hal Roach-M-G-M comedy.

Nurse your nickels until you get enough to see Charley Chase in "NICKEL NURSER," his latest Hal Roach-M-G-M comedy.

It shows good sense to spend a few cents to see Charley Chase in "NICKEL NURSER," a Hal Roach-M-G-M comedy.

THELMA TODD BACK WITH CHARLEY CHASE

Is Supported by Three Beautiful Blondes in Latest Hal Roach Comedy for M-G-M

Trying to find a suitable leading lady for a motion picture sometimes necessitates plenty of work, regardless of the number of talented artists in the film colony.

This was forcibly brought to the attention of executives when Charley Chase started preparations for the filming of "NICKEL NURSER," his latest Hal Roach-M-G-M comedy which comes..............to the..............Theatre.

So satisfactory had Thelma Todd proven in previous pictures with the comedian that she was wanted immediately by the star. The much-wanted blonde leading lady, however, was busy working on her own series of comedies with Zasu Pitts and the idea was temporarily abandoned.

A search was inaugurated for a girl of the same type as Thelma Todd, but after three weeks of exhaustive "tests" none of the girls met the requirements. During the interim Miss Todd completed the picture she had been working on with Zasu Pitts and was at liberty.

Although both Miss Todd and Charley Chase were under contract to the Hal Roach studios, Miss Todd was required to sign a new contract to play opposite the comedian. The intensive search was not entirely fruitless for three beautiful blondes, namely, Estelle Eterre, Hazel Howell and Geraldine D'vorak, were retained for prominent supporting roles. Billy Gilbert, rotund comedian character, is also in the cast. Warren Doane directed the comedy.

NEWSPAPER AD MATS FREE

HAL ROACH M-G-M present

CHARLEY CHASE

in his latest ALL-TALKING comedy "The Nickel Nurser"

HAL ROACH M-G-M present CHARLEY CHASE in his Latest Comedy

SHORT PARAGRAPHS

A coat of mail similar in design to those worn by the Knights in King Arthur's court plays an important part in the latest Charley Chase-Hal Roach comedy, "NICKEL NURSER," now playing at the..............Theatre. The suit, which weighed approximately 50 pounds, was made of a bronze, rust-proof metal vest and headgear with shoulder guards and solid metal leggings and legs and sleeves of a woven chain mesh of the same material. It was extremely warm, according to the actor, who lost three pounds while wearing it in the course of the picture.

"When ignorance is bliss it is folly

CHARLEY CHASE

to be wise." So thought a young property boy who, when he was asked to go to a costumer's shop for a coat of mail for Charley Chase, returned with a mail man's coat. He returned to the studio, however, after the second trip, with the desired armored suit which is seen in "NICKEL NURSER," the latest Hal Roach-M-G-M comedy which comes..............to the Theatre.

POSTERS

You can always tell an M-G-M poster by the distinctive and colorful flash with which it calls attention to the entertainment of the release which it advertises. These posters are typical examples of high-powered selling paper—for theatre front or general posting. The stock one sheet below is reproduced in rich purple rotogravure—all the effectiveness of direct photography.

SUBJECT 1 SHEET

EXPLOITATION POSSIBILITIES

ORDER YOUR ACCESSORIES EARLY!

Get the Benefit of Fresh Stock and Advance Advertising

YOU CAN
MAKE THIS
30 x 40
CUTOUT HEAD
FROM THE
3 SHEET POSTER

An extra use for the three sheet poster on the Charley Chase series is a large cutout head for use on the theatre marquee, lobby entrance stand or wall panel. A brilliant likeness of the popular comedian that makes a great flash for extra business. Mount the poster head on compo board, silhouette and put it to work. Properly exploited Chase is a favorite at all theatres.

STOCK ROTO 1 SHEET

8
11 x 14
LOBBY
DISPLAYS

These lobby displays are printed in rich sepia brown on heavy card stock and are especially adaptable for use in lobby display stands or wall panels. The eight cards of scenes and surrounding art are in themselves interesting and seat selling—their quality is a genuine asset of a business-building lobby.

(PRESS SHEET—SHIVER MY TIMBERS)

HAL ROACH presents

OUR GANG

A Boat Load of Laughs as Celebrated Rascals Cut Loose in Second Release of 10th Anniversary Series —

SHIVER MY TIMBERS

PRESS SHEET

A METRO-GOLDWYN-MAYER TALKING COMEDY

What to be When Grown Up Puzzles Our Gang

Future Success in Movies Seems Farthest From Thoughts of Roach-M-G-M Screen Stars

The mind of youth is fickle and not very comprehending.

Perhaps this may explain why, with brilliant futures before them, the little members of the famous Hal Roach Our Gang wish to be something besides screen stars when they grow up.

But their work is play to them and what youngster doesn't like to dream away some childish fancy?

The seriousness of their minds may be gathered from the answers given to the question of what they would like to be when they grow up.

Bobby "Wheezer" Hutchins is already paving the way to become a fireman. He has a fireman's outfit and when there is any lawn sprinkling to be done with the garden hose Bobby is usually on the nozzle end. And just let him hear a fire siren.

Dorothy "Echo" De Borba, a little lady of no small importance to Our Gang, expressed a desire to become a world traveler with no particular duties to perform. What is more fitting for a beautiful young lady?

An ambition to become a railroad engineer has overtaken little Mathew "Stymie" Beard and be one he will if his dreams come true. To be a great automobile racer is the job Sherwood "Spud" Bailey has cut out for himself, while Pete the Pup is quite satisfied to be an actor the rest of his life.

All the little youngsters, regardless of their dreams, will be seen in "SHIVER MY TIMBERS," the latest Hal Roach - M-G-M comedy which comes . . . . to the . . . . Theatre. Robert McGowan directed the picture.

PUBLICITY

SHORT PARAGRAPHS

Believe it or not, June Marlowe receives fan mail addressed to Miss Crabtree. Making her introduction to Our Gang fans as Miss Crabtree in the role of a school teacher, the character name has branded her as a trade mark. Many of her youthful followers even speak to her on the street as Miss Crabtree. Her role in "SHIVER MY TIMBERS," the latest Hal Roach-M-G-M comedy coming to the . . . . Theatre next . . . ., marks her fourth appearance with Our Gang under the original character name.

It is doubtful if any of the tiny members of Our Gang will ever become seamen. Practically all of the burly sailors seen in "SHIVER MY TIMBERS," the latest Hal Roach-M-G-M comedy now playing at the . . . . Theatre, were at one time dyed-in-the-wool seamen. Some served in the late war. During their idle moments while making the picture they would relate their experiences to the youngsters and all of them agreed they would much rather stay in Hollywood and make pictures.

There is some advantage in being a member of Our Gang other than the fact that the children warrant more attention than adult players on the Hal Roach lot. They don't have to wear make-up, and take it from any screen player who has to daub make-up on before being photographed, it is some item. It is not only a financial benefit, but the time and trouble saved by not using grease paint makes the youngsters the envy of most players. The latest Our Gang comedy, "SHIVER MY TIMBERS," is now playing at the . . . . Theatre.

A strange alley cat played the role of a pursuer pursued in a little off-stage comedy during the filming of "SHIVER MY TIMBERS," the latest Hal Roach-M-G-M-Our Gang comedy now playing at the Theatre. While enacting a scene Pete the Pup espied a strange cat stalking a mouse on the set. With one yelp he made a lunge for the feline intruder and chased her off the stage. He was brought back very shortly by his owner, thoroughly reprimanded.

Wearing of rain coats to keep dry indoors is unusual anywhere, but more so perhaps in California. But that is precisely what took place on a sound stage at the Hal Roach Studios while filming "SHIVER MY TIMBERS," the latest Our Gang comedy now playing at the . . . . Theatre. In one sequence of the picture depicting a terrible storm at sea, several men splashed 365 gallons of water over two huge boxes containing the youngsters. In order to keep dry, Director Robert McGowan and his staff of assistants were forced to don waterproof apparel.

SYNOPSIS

As an old sea captain spins fantastic and lavishly embellished tales of pirates and shipwrecks for the amusement of "Our Gang," the little rascals decide to play "hookey" from school and become sailors. "Echo" endeavors to get her classmates back to their studies, but when they refuse she goes to tell the teacher what has happened. The teacher, who has had several such experiences, goes to the dock to see if the captain will help her in getting the youngsters to school. The captain is only too willing and explains a plan that will cure the kiddies of ever following the sea. He asks the children if they would like to leave with him on a voyage the next day and they thrill with the thought. The following day they board the ship dressed in various pirate outfits and sea-going togs. As part of his plan the skipper immediately gets very rough with his men and knocks several of them down with his whip, which he lashes about in fury. The children become scared, but at the skipper's command they go below, where a regular fight is staged for their benefit. Unknown to the children the ship is still docked, but suddenly one of the sailors reports a terrible storm at sea and the skipper tells the children to climb into the hold of the ship. With the help of his men he splashes water on the boxes and produces a regular "rough sea." Finally he brings in the teacher and tells the children that he has kidnapped her and that all of them are about to fall into the hands of a pirate ship. The children are fully scared of the sea by this time and they promise the teacher they will go back to school as they chase the "pirate" sailors from the ship.

LIFE NOT ALL WORK FOR OUR GANG

Plenty of Time for the Sports That All Kids Love

Practically everyone has some pet sport or diversion.

It is only natural then that members of the famous Hal Roach "Our Gang" would show partiality in their pastimes. When not at work in a picture they may generally be found amusing themselves thusly:

Bobby "Wheezer" Hutchins riding a "scooter bike."

Dorothy "Echo" De Borba playing with her dolls in a lady-like manner.

Sherwood "Spud" Bailey giving his neighborhood baseball team a work-out.

Mathew "Stymie" Beard playing marbles.

Pete the Pup chasing cats.

And Director Robert McGowan playing golf.

All the little members of Our Gang are playing at the . . . . Theatre in "SHIVER MY TIMBERS," their latest Hal Roach comedy. June Marlowe and Billy Gilbert are seen in supporting roles of the picture.

MEMBERS OF OUR GANG DISTINCT PERSONALITIES

Each Has Some Feature by Which He Is Readily Identified

Like the trade mark on sterling silver, practically all movie personalities have some peculiar mark or expression that stamps their identity.

Many have exercised to advantage their particular "trade mark" until they are known the world over as the sole owners. There is Greta Garbo's languid eyes, Jean Harlow's platinum blonde hair, Charlie Chaplin's moustache and scores of other markings which identify their owners.

For years screen fans have been seeing the little members of "Our Gang," and although new faces are seen in the group from time to time, each has some "trade mark."

Perhaps the best established in Our Gang is the black ring around the left eye of Pete the Pup.

Then, of course, there is the smiling, cherubic face of Bobby "Wheezer" Hutchins, the pretty blonde curls and dimples of Dorothy "Echo" De Borba, the red hair and freckles of Sherwood "Spud" Bailey and, last but not least, the ivory white teeth of Mathew "Stymie" Beard shining from his cute but colored countenance.

You can tell if you remember them when you see "SHIVER MY TIMBERS," the latest Hal Roach-M-G-M comedy featuring Our Gang, now playing at the . . . . Theatre. Robert McGowan directed the picture, which has in supporting roles June Marlowe and Billy Gilbert.

A HAL ROACH-M-G-M-OUR GANG COMEDY

"SHIVER MY TIMBERS"

Starring
Our Gang

Director
Robert McGowan

Cameraman
Art Lloyd

Story Editor
H. M. Walker

Film Editor
Richard Currier

Sound Engineer
Elmer Raguse

A Victor Recording
Western Electric System
FOOTAGE—1873
RUNNING TIME—21 Minutes

SHORT PARAGRAPHS

The making of sea pictures is not always a pleasant outing as members of the Hal Roach Our Gang can testify. During the filming of "SHIVER MY TIMBERS," which comes . . . . to the . . . . Theatre, practically all the little youngsters were stricken with seasickness. Although the ship on which they worked was docked, constant rolling of the ocean created enough of the "at sea" sensation to upset the children.

San Pedro, the largest seaport on the Pacific Coast, was used as a location for "SHIVER MY TIMBERS," the Hal Roach-M-G-M-Our Gang comedy which comes . . . . to the . . . . Theatre. Many of the world's largest steamers and foreign import vessels dock within a stone's throw of where

OUR GANG

the scenes were filmed. Many of the boxes, bales and barrels seen in the picture were marked for export to the far corners of the globe.

A willingness to play and please gave Pete the Pup, canine member of Our Gang, the greatest scare of his career. While filming some of the scenes for "SHIVER MY TIMBERS" on the pier at San Pedro one of the youngsters threw a stick into the water some thirty feet below. Pete plunged into the water and retrieved the missle, but the waves were so strong he had considerable difficulty in reaching shore. Complete exhaustion was the only ill effect, however. The picture opens next . . . . at the . . . . Theatre.

Take it from an old-time stowaway —the sea is no place for children, especially if they ship with the idea of becoming pirates or treasure hunters. Members of Our Gang received this information first hand from Billy Gilbert, who plays the role of a sea captain with them in "SHIVER MY TIMBERS," the latest Hal Roach-M-G-M comedy which comes . . . . to the . . . . Theatre. At the age of seven Gilbert took a turn at the sea as a stowaway. He was returned to his parents a sadder but wiser child after three days on the briny deep. Hence his advice.

CATCHLINES

Shiver my timbers if it isn't Hal Roach's Our Gang in "SHIVER MY TIMBERS."

* * *

If you are all at sea see Our Gang in "SHIVER MY TIMBERS," a Hal Roach comedy.

* * *

You don't have to be a sailor to see Our Gang in "SHIVER MY TIMBERS," a Hal Roach comedy.

* * *

If you want to go out to sea in gales of laughter see Our Gang in "SHIVER MY TIMBERS," a Hal Roach comedy.

* * *

Man the laugh boats! Our Gang in "SHIVER MY TIMBERS," a Hal Roach comedy.

* * *

You'll shiver with laughter when you see Our Gang in "SHIVER MY TIMBERS," a Hal Roach comedy.

* * *

Walk the gang plank with Our Gang in "SHIVER MY TIMBERS," a Hal Roach comedy.

OUR GANG "REGULAR FELLERS" AT SPORT

Hal Roach's Screen Rascals Have Favorite Pastimes

If there are any little youngsters in the world who think that members of Our Gang aren't "regular fellers," they should see these potential stars off the screen.

Working in pictures doesn't mean a thing to them.

In fact they are as much themselves while in the studio as they are at home, for it's all play to them.

Between scenes they may be seen riding "skooter bikes" or playing games on vacant stages and most of them bring toys from home to amuse themselves. A huge sand box is conveniently located in the studio, where all of them may be found at various times enjoying life with the cares of picture making forgotten.

Pete the Pup, canine member of the group, is perhaps the most playful of all. He no sooner finishes a scene than he is up to some trick with his little playmates.

Even Director Robert McGowan enters in the youthful spirit of his pictures and enters in many games the youngsters play on the sets. Hide-and-seek is perhaps the most popular of their indoor sports, for picture stages offer hundreds of places for the children to conceal themselves.

They were given an opportunity to play their favorite game in "SHIVER MY TIMBERS," the latest Hal Roach-M-G-M comedy which comes . . . . to the . . . . Theatre. June Marlowe and Billy Gilbert, other members of the cast, also enter in the game.

Newspaper Ad Mats

Two small ad mats that can be used individually or which can easily be dropped in a corner of your larger space newspaper ads. Equally suitable for program announcements, etc. Our Gang Comedies mean extra money at any box office—it's up to you to get behind them with every available accessory.

Ask for these mats at your M-G-M Exchange—FREE

COMPLETE ADVERTISING ACCESSORIES THAT MAKE EXPLOITATION EASY AND EFFECTIVE

Press Sheet
Subject One Sheet
Subject Three Sheet
Stock One Sheet (rotogravure)
1 Scene Mat (stock) — FREE
2 Ad Mats (stock) — FREE
8—11x14 Lobby Cards
10—Black and White Photos

ORDER FROM YOUR
M-G-M EXCHANGE

POSTERS

You can always tell an M-G-M poster by the distinctive and colorful flash with which it calls attention to the entertainment of the release which it advertises. These posters are typical examples of high-powered selling

SUBJECT 1 SHEET

SUBJECT 3 SHEET

paper—for theatre front or general posting. The stock one sheet below is reproduced in rich blue rotogravure—all the effectiveness of direct photography.

STOCK 1 SHEET

8
11 x 14
LOBBY
DISPLAYS

Use these eight cards for a frame display in your lobby or on your theatre front. They depict interesting scenes from this particular picture—scenes of Our Gang that say "come in" to passersby.

These display cards are photo-gelatined in rich sepia brown on extra heavy stock with the result that the appeal of the picture is put over in a manner that can scarcely be achieved in any other way. At your M-G-M Exchange.

Jerry Tucker (Jerry Schatz) is the young boy in the back of this photo from "Mama's Little Pirate." "Shiver My Timbers" was his first appearance with Our Gang.

Dorthy De Borba, another Gang member who appeared in "Shiver My Timbers" posed for this publicity still. "Shiver My Timbers" was her 11th appearance in the Our Gang series.

MOVIE PUBLICITY SHOWCASE VOLUME 1

LAUREL & HARDY IN "SWISS MISS"

I. JOSEPH HYATT

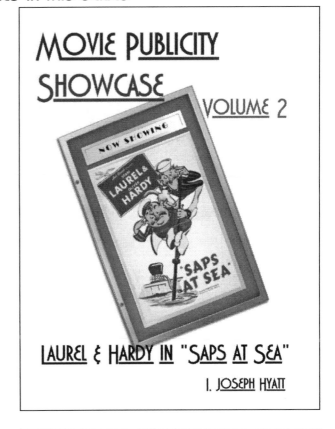

MOVIE PUBLICITY SHOWCASE VOLUME 2

LAUREL & HARDY IN "SAPS AT SEA"

I. JOSEPH HYATT

MOVIE PUBLICITY SHOWCASE VOLUME 3

OLIVER HARDY & HARRY LANGDON IN "ZENOBIA"
BY I. JOSEPH HYATT

MOVIE PUBLICITY SHOWCASE VOLUME 4

LAUREL & HARDY IN "THE FLYING DEUCES" & "UTOPIA"
BY I. JOSEPH HYATT

MOVIE PUBLICITY
SHOWCASE

VOLUME 5

LAUREL AND HARDY IN "SONS OF THE DESERT"
BY I. JOSEPH HYATT

COMING DECEMBER 2015

MOVIE PUBLICITY
SHOWCASE

VOLUME 7

LAUREL & HARDY IN "OUR RELATIONS"
BY I. JOSEPH HYATT

ABOUT THE AUTHOR

I. Joseph Hyatt is an entertainment archeologist. A member of the Sons of the Desert, the Laurel and Hardy Appreciation Society, Hyatt's articles have been printed internationally. Traveling across the US, and drawing on many collections, including his own, he brings back past eras with words and photographs.

His first book, "Stan Laurel's Valet - The Jimmy Murphy Story" was based on his close friendship with Jimmy Murphy. While a biography of one of the world's most entertaining valets, it's focus includes the 1940-42 US theatrical tours of Laurel and Hardy.

"Life and Death of a Movie Theater" tells the story of a small town theater and its competition from the depression through the war years, the television years and through to the current day.

He has also written "Hollywood Victory Caravan" which describes the USA's largest bond tour during the war years. Rare private home movie frames capture and recreate the entire show. Travel with the troupe to all 12 cities. Extra information includes the Mexico pre-show and the San Francisco post-show. Souvenir programs from Bob Hope, Oliver Hardy and Charles Boyer are reproduced along with ticket stubs, crew badges, advertising and publicity photos. Stars include (in alphabetical order) Desi Arnaz, Joan Blondell, Joan Bennett, Charles Boyer, James Cagney, Claudette Colbert, Jerry Colonna, Bing Crosby, Olivia de Havilland, Cary Grant, Charlotte Greenwood, Bob Hope (as Master of Ceremonies), Bert Lahr, Frances Langford, Stan Laurel and Oliver Hardy, Groucho Marx, Frank McHugh, Ray Middleton, Merle Oberon, Pat O'Brien, Eleanor Powell, Rise Stevens, and many more! Available in Color or Black and White editions.

Other books by I. Joseph Hyatt:

Movie Publicity Showcase Volume 1: Laurel and Hardy in "Swiss Miss"
Movie Publicity Showcase Volume 2: Laurel and Hardy in "Saps at Sea"
Movie Publicity Showcase Volume 3: Oliver Hardy and Harry Langdon in "Zenobia"
Movie Publicity Showcase Volume 4: Laurel and Hardy in "The Flying Deuces" & "Utopia"
Movie Publicity Showcase Volume 5: Laurel and Hardy in "Sons of the Desert"
Movie Publicity Showcase Volume 6: Laurel and Hardy in "Thicker Than Water" and other short subjects
Coming in December 2015
Movie Publicity Showcase Volume 7: Laurel and Hardy in "Our Relations"

The Movie Publicity Showcase series places movies into their historical "first run" context, utilizing original press material from the time of their release, and subsequent theatrical revivals. Read about your favorite stars as they were during the day of the movie's initial release. See how creative theater managers could draw in an audience when movie exhibition was an art form. Step back into time and see what movie fans of that day experienced when going to the movies!

49010685R00041

Made in the USA
Middletown, DE
03 October 2017